How to Keep Your Woman Happy; A Manual for Men

by Skye Hasson

1663 LIBERTY DRIVE, SUITE 200
BLOOMINGTON, INDIANA 47403
(800) 839-8640
WWW.AUTHORHOUSE.COM

This book is a work of non-fiction. Unless otherwise noted, the author and the publisher make no explicit guarantees as to the accuracy of the information contained in this book and in some cases, names of people and places have been altered to protect their privacy.

© 2005 Skye Hasson. All Rights Reserved.

No part of this book may be reproduced, stored in a retrieval system, or transmitted by any means without the written permission of the author.

First published by AuthorHouse 10/31/05

ISBN: 1-4208-5053-9 (sc)

Library of Congress Control Number: 2005903991

Printed in the United States of America
Bloomington, Indiana

This book is printed on acid-free paper.

Several helpful women and good-natured men contributed to this manual. I especially thank Kelly Martin, Vicky Mantzey, Ken Mantzey, Kyla Hardesty, Des Bergsing, and Alyce Ross.

For my husband Kelly,
who inspired this book
partially because of the things he does so well,
and partially because of the things he doesn't do, so well.

A note to "new-age, sensitive" guys:

This book may not work as well for you. Your partner, if she is female, may be more interested in having you read something like The Art of Belching, Spitting, and Chewing Tobacco, or Being Macho for Dummies. The fact is that, although most women want their men to be sweet, thoughtful, and attuned to their every need, they also want them to be strong, confident, and "manly" (whatever that means). You probably already do all the things described in this book and then some. So, if you're the kind of guy who always remembers birthdays, anniversaries, and special occasions; easily talks about his feelings (note "easily"); and are constantly at her beck and call when she's sick, then put this book back on the shelf. Go buy something else. She's just not going to appreciate it.

TABLE OF CONTENTS

A note to "new-age, sensitive" guys ix

Introduction xiii

Dating 1

Day-to-Day Tips 7

When She's Sick 13

When She's Upset 21

When She's Upset With You 27

When You're Upset 37

Jealousy and Double Standards 43

Proposing 49

Birthdays, Valentine's Day, Anniversaries, and Other Special Occasions 55

In Bed 65

Household 73

General Helpful Hints 79

Conclusion 85

Introduction

There are many good reasons to learn how to keep your woman happy. The first, of course, is simply that you love her and that you *want* her to be happy. Even though you may be strong and tough, sometimes dense, occasionally unfeeling, and generally kind of oblivious, you do actually care about the woman you're with and want her to feel good about herself and her life (not to mention you).

Secondly, if you have any concerns about whether she will stay with you as long as you may want her to, you realize that it is a good idea to give her as many reasons as possible to stick around. That involves having her think you're a great guy.

Thirdly, take it from Deuce Bigalow: "If you make a woman feel good about herself, it doesn't matter what's wrong with you." If you have any concerns about your own attractiveness, physically or simply as a human being, keeping your woman happy is the best way to keep her attracted to you.

And lastly, it is frequently the case that when one person in a relationship is making a distinct effort to provide contentment for his or her partner, the other person, feeling loved and cherished, begins to return the effort. This dynamic can easily lead to pleasant, low-hassle interactions, helping a man to live the life he really wants (one with a minimum of nagging and being complained and whined at, and a maximum of peace, relaxation, and ease of living).

It is common knowledge that the sexes do not understand each other. Well, it may be that some women think they understand men, and some men think they understand women, but they are both wrong. Anyway, it is no shame to admit that your woman baffles you; it's probably even cool (macho, whatever). You may find yourself constantly confused. You may realize that you will probably never fully understand women. But, if it is important to you to make an effort to please her, and to have some idea of the right thing to do in a given situation, then this book is for you.

The suggestions in this book are just that: suggestions. All women are different. Although it is likely that your significant other will appreciate and agree with many of the ideas offered here (in fact, she may have just handed the book over and demanded that you read it from cover to cover immediately), perhaps you will come across a comment that doesn't fit your partner at all. If you are sure that you are correct (and you can never be too careful about checking whether you are or not) feel free to cross that item out. Or, if she knows about the book, you may even want to have her go through it, crossing things out and adding her own observations where necessary. For this purpose, several blank pages have been inserted between sections.

Dating

- **Bring flowers.** Even if it is your first date, you can never go wrong with flowers. She'll immediately think you are a thoughtful, considerate kind of guy who definitely deserves a chance.

    Note: flowers may be store bought, but an even more thoughtful and romantic gesture is to pick them yourself. At least remove the plastic wrapper.

- **Dress nicely.** A torn t-shirt, even a clean t-shirt, is not going to impress her. She'll feel as if she just isn't important enough for you to go to that extra effort.

- **Call if you are going to be late.** Women consider this common courtesy; even if you are doing something really important that cannot be interrupted. No, she will not understand.

- **Do not take her to McDonalds.** If you cannot afford to take her someplace better than a fast food joint, then make her dinner or take her out for dessert instead. Fast food is like a torn t-shirt.

    (The only exception to this rule is if you have been dating for a while and you know, without a doubt, that she happens to love McDonalds. Or, if she has kids that will enjoy Playland.)

- **Make conversation.** Try not to talk too much about yourself, and certainly do not mention your past girlfriends. At the same time, feel free to tell short stories, especially funny ones, about yourself or your family or your job. Most importantly, ask her questions about herself. When a man asks questions about a woman, the woman feels that he is honestly interested in getting to know her. She feels that he cares about who she really is.

- **Call her the next day.** Even if you're not ready to go on another date, call her and let her know that you had a good time. She will think of you as unusually confident and thoughtful.

- **Make a big deal out of Valentine's Day.** The average woman has spent many sad Valentine's Days watching her friends have romantic experiences with their partners and feeling lonely and left out. Having a partner who invests thought and caring into the day can be very fulfilling for a woman. Even if you are newly dating, it is easy to do something small that will mean a lot to her, but not necessarily indicate a major commitment from you. See **Birthdays, Valentine's Day, Anniversaries, and Other Special Occasions** for ideas.

If she has kids:

- **Do not pretend to like them.** They will know. She will probably know. Try to honestly like them. If you can't, maybe there isn't much hope for the relationship.

- **Bring the kids little presents.** Especially if you bring her something. They feel included, and she sees you as considerate and generous. Don't be excessive, though, or else they and she may feel as if you are trying to buy their affection. Little candies, small toy cars or dolls, stickers and magic markers can go a long way without having too much of an impact on your wallet.

- **Consider them when going out.** If you can manage a date with the kids, take everyone to a family place they will enjoy. Consider Chuck E. Cheese or McDonalds. Let her know that you realize that she is a package deal.

- **Offer to pay for the kids** if you include them on an outing. Or, better yet, just pay for them without offering.

- **If you have been dating long enough,** arrange for a babysitter when you want to go out alone. Also, offer to take responsibility for paying for and taking the sitter home.

Day-to-Day Tips

- **Ask her how her day was.** Listening is one of the most important things you can do for a woman. Even if absolutely nothing happened to her, she wants to know that you care enough to listen to every (maybe even boring) detail. Your attentive silence and occasional relevant questions tell a woman, "You are important to me. I care about every minute of your day because I care so much about you." Questions that have to do with what she has just been talking about add a great deal. They are proof to her that you are actually listening to what she is saying. They tell her, "I want to help you work through this," or, "What an interesting woman you are!" If you are watching television or reading something, demonstrate the depth of your interest by turning off the TV or putting away your reading material. This will say more to her about how much you think of her than any other single act. Also, try to maintain eye contact. Women often feel that if you are not looking at them then you can't possibly be listening to what they are saying. Definitely do not fall asleep or respond with "Uh-huh," "What did you say?" "Yes, Dear," or, "Would you be quiet? This is my favorite part of the show."

- **Tell her about *your* day.** It is often rare for men to offer information. A real treat for a woman, odd as it may seem, is to hear how your day went. Even just a short summary of the highlights will express to a woman that you enjoy talking, sharing, and just being with her. It will also imply that her presence and opinions are important to you. This makes a woman feel valued and loved.

    However, do not interrupt her with your own stories while she is telling you about *her* day. If you must, then tie your own story back to whatever she was saying and encourage her to go on when you've finished. Otherwise, she will begin to feel that you consider the events in your life far more important than the events in hers. (You may very well feel that way, but it is not in your best interest to communicate that.)

- **Revive chivalry.** This suggestion must be treated with caution because nowadays there are women that will take offense at having a door opened, the check paid, or the bags carried for them. However, there are also many women who will appreciate such acts of consideration and recognize you as a true gentleman for thinking of them. Sincere sexism is no longer as common as it once was. Chances are that a woman will feel pampered rather than insulted.

    Gallant gestures include those mentioned above, as well as:
    - always walk to her outside (so that if a passing car sprays mud you will be the victim, rather than she);
    - lift or move heavy objects for her;
    - complete small repair jobs for her;
    - always open a door for her, even the car door;
    - call the waiter over if she desires something; and
    - introduce her when encountering an acquaintance of yours that she does not know.

- **Be romantic.** Many men are unclear on the true import of romance. For women, little acts can mean a great deal. Any one of the following will remind her how much you appreciate her presence in your life.

    Some examples include:
    - holding her hand in public;
    - buying her spur-of-the moment flowers;
    - leaving her a love note;
    - writing her a letter when you're away;
    - giving her a card that you have made or written in;
    - kissing her when you arrive and when you leave;
    - expressing, in words, how you feel about her;
    - bringing her chocolates wrapped in a red bow;
    - winking at her from across the room at a party;

- o   dancing with her in the living room; and
- o   singing her love songs.

These acts are not corny to a woman. They are an effective way to show her how much you think of her and how precious she is to you.

- **Stand up for her.** This is especially important in two ways:
    1) If she is involved in a heated argument, and it is appropriate to give your opinion, try to take her side. Do not lie if you disagree with her, but if you can honestly reiterate her perspective, do so firmly and without embarrassment. If you do not agree with her, find something to say that might deflate the tension and at the same time will support her. She will feel championed by you and respected, as well as more confident about standing up for herself. This is especially important in situations involving family members.
    2) If she is in a situation that requires assertiveness (for instance, if someone is harassing her or trying to take advantage of her in some way) help her to take whatever steps necessary. Help her by making suggestions, validating her feelings, and encouraging her to take action (not by taking over the situation yourself). If she actually requests your help, step in and take care of it. (Many women may be annoyed by this suggestion and may even be angry at you if you act on it. However, plenty of women do not consider this a sexist attitude, merely appropriate and protective behavior. Be sure to find out how your partner feels.)

- **Date her.** If you have been seeing each other for a while and spend most of your time together just hanging out watching TV, ask her on a date. Surprise her with a full picnic basket or take her to dinner and a movie. This will remind her that the reason you *can* "just" hang out with her is because she is so special to you.

When She's Sick

When She's Sick

A man who knows how to take care of a woman when she is sick is considered by women to be a tremendous asset. Proper attention during this time suggests to a woman that, though perhaps gruff, unsympathetic, and insensitive on the outside, you actually have a nurturing and loving inside. And, even though many women do prefer a strong masculine type of man, they also want to occasionally experience a caring and attentive type.

- **Ask her if she needs anything** several times a day. If you are away from the house, then be sure to call.

- **Give her the remote control.** Even if you are home and want to watch TV. She's sick. She deserves to watch what she wants.

- **Bring her anything she asks for** (within reason, of course), as well as things she does not ask for. For instance:
    - If she has a cold, be sure to buy cough drops, chicken broth, orange juice, and those tissues with aloe in them.
    - If she has a fever, put a cool wet towel on her forehead.
    - If it is her time of the month, gently massage her lower back.
    - Try to keep her stocked up with movies she hasn't seen. (Movies of the type that *she* likes, not that *you* like.)

- **Make her tea.** Only if she likes it, naturally. Many women will enjoy a cup of tea suited to whatever is ailing her. These days it is easy to pick up sore throat tea, digestion tea, fever tea, or whatever an ill person might need. Even if she doesn't drink it, the idea that you thought of it and took the time to prepare it will do wonders. Hint: add a little honey. All teas taste better with honey.

- **Fix meals for her without being asked.** (But make sure she's hungry first or it will be a waste of your time and effort). Try to keep them nutritious: include a meat, a starch, and a vegetable (anything green should be top on your list – spinach, chard, broccoli...). For nausea, though, stick with saltine crackers, or toast. TV dinners, macaroni and cheese, pizza, or other quick meals are not advisable, except when absolutely unavoidable.

- **Let her stay in bed.** Do anything she feels obligated to get up and do. Whether she is *that* sick or not, it will make her feel cared for and treasured. Aside from earning you brownie points, such actions, and her emotional response to them, will produce a quicker recovery. This means feeding the kids or pets, buying groceries, washing the dishes, etc.

- **Bring her presents.** Get-well presents are highly underrated (at least when you are an under-the-weather woman and they are from your man). Presents demonstrate that you are thinking about her and that you care that she is miserable. They do not have to be expensive; a card with some personal sentiment scrawled inside is probably one of the best bets, though flowers and stuffed animals work well, too.

  Other options:
    - a balloon or two;
    - a scented candle;
    - bubble bath;
    - skin lotion;
    - a single rose in a vase;
    - a comfortable nightshirt...
    - use your imagination or suggestions from a helpful female store clerk (who will think you are the sweetest guy she has ever met).

- **Keep the house clean.** This may be hard, but usually it's only for a short time, and it will earn you unbelievable brownie points. However, be careful about overdoing it. Too much cleaning will make her feel as if you are afraid of her germs. And if she has a migraine, do not vacuum.

- In her room:
  - keep the bedside area as neat and uncluttered as possible;
  - empty the trash;
  - clean up her tissues; and
  - do the laundry.
- In the rest of the house:
  - vacuum;
  - dust;
  - mop the floors;
  - make sure the dishes are done; and
  - basically clean up any mess that she is going to worry about and feel stressed over (on top of being sick).

And as soon as she is feeling better, wash the bed-sheets. There's nothing worse than finally feeling better and then climbing back into your bed of sickness.

- **Do not make her feel as if she is a leper.** If being around sick people is a real problem for you, then fake it. An already under-the-weather woman will feel even worse if she begins feeling rejected by you. Disgusted or inattentive behavior on your part will produce exaggerated emotional responses on her part. Negative ones. Directed at you, her life in general, and anything else she can think of. She may become unreasonably depressed, or even slightly hysterical. The effort required to prevent this will be worthwhile in the long run.

- **Do not avoid her.** Making excuses to be out of the house, or hanging out with your buddies while she is miserable will likely cause all of the reactions mentioned above. She is likely to say to herself: "He doesn't really care about me. He only wants to be with me when I'm fun to be around. I'm not important enough to him for him to show any concern. I'm unlovable." And so on. Again, a wiser course is to grin and bear it.

- **Do NOT ask her to do things that she is not up to doing.** A woman will often (believe it or not) go to incredible lengths to keep her man happy, including grocery shopping when she is too sick to do so, ironing, doing laundry, feeding the pets or kids, and anything else her man is too self-absorbed to take care of himself. Even a well-meaning invitation out to lunch or dinner can actually put unnecessary pressure on her.

- **Tell her that you love her.** A woman feels most unattractive when her hair is a mess, she hasn't showered, and she is lying in dirty sheets, surrounded by byproducts of her body's attempts to heal itself. This is when saying "I love you" can mean the most.

- **If there are kids, take them for the day,** or at least part of the day. As much time as possible. It is challenging to be a mother any day, how much more so when you are sick?

- **If you are at work,** or otherwise unavoidably away from her for the day, call her several times to see how she's feeling. Even if you are worried that she is sleeping, it will be more important to her to know that you care about how she is doing.

When She's Upset

- **Ask her if she wants to talk.** The answer will always be "yes." Even if she says "no," it's "yes." So, if she does refuse, ask her again. Try to rephrase it. Here are some options: "I'd like to hear about it," "I can tell something is bothering you," "I really want to help if I can," "What did you think of what just happened?" or "It's really bothering you a lot, isn't it?" She may say "no" three or four times, but keep at it. Be strong. Be persistent. A woman wants to know that you truly want to hear what she is feeling and thinking. She wants you to insist so that she will not feel as if she is burdening you with her problems, or taking you away from something you feel is more important. (Of course, if there *is* something you find more important than your upset woman – which is what she will think if you do not convince her to talk – this will upset her even further.)

  However, there are women who prefer to be left alone when they are upset. This is when a conversation ahead of time, before anything ever happens, is a good idea. Know your woman's preferences before these situations arise. Be prepared.

- **Stick around.** Your presence alone will let her know that you care. If you leave, she will be certain that her emotional state is of no importance to you whatsoever (even though you have probably done it out of respect for what you judge to be her need to be left alone). What she sees as your abandonment of her will lead to her feeling even worse. It is quite possible that she will become even more upset by what she perceives as your rejection than she had been about the original situation.

- **Let her vent.** Just listen to her for as long as she wants, even if it's boring, even if it's about her friends or her work or the neighbors, even if it's upsetting you, even if it's about your mother or your dog or your job. She just needs to get it out of her system. If all you do is listen quietly and nod occasionally, you will be amazed at how validated and loved she will feel. In fact, just expressing it without being judged or argued with by you, may resolve the issue for her completely.

- **Validate her.** Find something about what she is saying to agree with. Anything. Make sympathetic noises and gestures. If there is nothing you can agree with, tell her that you understand how she feels.

- **Let her cry.** Women sometimes need to cry. It's not the end of the world. Just be there. Hold her or rub her back. Tell her that you love her, and that it's going to be okay. Don't rush her.

- **Do not try to fix it.** As the author John Gray so wisely publicized, women often do not want or need you to come up with a solution. If you come up with one, bite your tongue. She needs to talk about it, to have a conversation with someone who is interested and concerned, not a quick fix.

  The exception to this rule is that once she has calmed down, if she seems to want a clear solution, then you may make suggestions. If she doesn't take them, try not to feel frustrated, it just means that she did not really want them in the first place.

- **Tell her what you think.** Especially if you agree with her, but even if you don't. Don't be defensive or attacking, just calmly and gently share your opinion. Part of the way women cope is through a verbal exchange. It would be very helpful if you thought of a similar situation to tell her about, including, hopefully, how it was resolved. You can end your story by asking, "Is that how you feel?" or "Does that sound like your experience?" This tells her that you are not talking just to talk, you are talking because you are hearing her and trying to understand where she is coming from.

- **Hold her.** Put your hand on her back or shoulder. Hug her. Touching her reminds her that no matter what she is saying or how she is coming across, you love her and respect where she is coming from.

- **When you think she has calmed down sufficiently,** you can ask her if she feels any better. If she smiles or laughs while she says no, you're okay. Hug her again. Tell her that you love her. If you can, offer to do something with her for the rest of the day. This will mean to her that you love her even when she is sad and needy, and that it is important to you to be there for her whenever she needs you. (In all likelihood, you will not get stuck doing something you would really rather not for the entire afternoon. It is the offer that counts, and she will rarely take advantage of it – unless, of course, her emotional state really does require it.)

When She's Upset With You

- **Do not try to avoid a discussion.** Bringing her presents, pretending nothing is wrong, or trying to solve it with sex is unlikely to be effective. Most often such responses will only frustrate and anger her more.

- **Try to address the situation immediately,** even though it may be the last thing you want to deal with. The longer she stays angry the worse it is going to be for you when it does get dealt with. Also, a major reason that women leave their partners is a partner's lack of communication skills. Letting her stew for an hour, or even days, is doing yourself no favor. Guaranteed, she is not going to "just get over it."

- **Do not leave.** <u>Even if she tells you to.</u> There are men (who have not read the aforementioned John Gray) that believe women want to be left alone when they are upset, especially when they are upset with their men. In reality, the exact opposite is usually true. It is very important for a man to understand that a woman practically never wants you to leave her alone. **When a man walks away from a woman who is unhappy, she feels abandoned, unloved, rejected, pathetic, and increasingly miserable.** Anyway, she is not going to feel better until she is able to *talk* about it with you in a satisfactory way. Until she feels that it is *resolved*. If she tells you to leave, it is because she wants you to prove that this is so important to you that you will stay anyway. So if you can handle it, stick around. Things will work out more quickly and smoothly that way.

- **Never tell her, "Well, I don't know what to say,"** or "I just can't think of anything to say," or "What do you want me to say?" You may be in all honesty just expressing how you are feeling and you actually can't think of anything to say that will make the situation better. But what *she* hears is: "This situation is ridiculous. You are upset for no reason. You are making a big deal out of nothing. I'm tired of it and, as soon as you let me, I'm going to leave you alone until you get over it." Or "I don't know how to fix this so I'm not going to even try. You are the one with the problem so you'll just have to figure it out for the both of us." If any of these statements describe your actual opinions, you may be in the wrong relationship (in fact, you may not be ready to be in a relationship at all.)

- **Do not ask her, "What's wrong?"** or "Are you upset about something?" A woman wants you to telepathically divine that something is wrong. Especially if it is something that you have done. Such a question will only upset her more, leading her to such thoughts as: "Why doesn't he care enough about me to have noticed what is upsetting me?" and "He thinks I'm overreacting." <u>Try not to indicate that you have no idea why she is suddenly pouting or crying.</u>

- **The best thing you can do is figure out why she is upset without asking her.** If you do know what is bothering her, then apologize thoroughly, summarizing what you did wrong, why she has the right to be upset, and why you would be upset in the same situation. She will be a little annoyed that she did not get to vent, and may still express her feelings for a while. Mostly, though, she will be astonished at your depth of understanding and self-awareness, not to mention consideration of her and her feelings.

- **Invite her to talk.** This is, of course, in almost any situation, the smartest course of action with a woman. First, demonstrate that you know and care that she is upset. Comments like: "You're pretty upset, huh?" or, "I screwed up, didn't I?" will show that you are in touch with her feelings and prepared to hear her express them. If she doesn't immediately respond, encourage her by saying something like: "Let's talk about it," or, a gentle, "Tell me what you're thinking." Turn off the TV or put away your magazine, and give her your full attention. The sooner you start this part, the sooner it will be over.

- **Do not say, "I'm sorry"** before she has calmed down. It will not do any good and you will have wasted your apology. As a result, when you say that you're sorry later, when she's ready for it, she won't believe that you mean it.

- **Do not say, "I'll never do it again,"** because chances are that you will and she knows it. She will only feel that you are trying to make the problem go away without *resolving* it. This will lead her to feel that you don't care about her feelings, that the relationship is not that important to you, and that maybe it's time for a parting of the ways.

- **Do not make excuses.** Do not try to talk your way out of her anger. Not only will she not listen, but she will only become more and more angry. Whether her fury is valid or not, your rationalizations will suggest to her that you have no intention of taking her feelings seriously.

- **Do not dismiss her feelings.** Never tell an upset woman that she is being ridiculous. Every emotion a woman experiences is, in one way or another, significant to her. She needs to know that if something is important to her, than it is equally important to you, simply because *she* is important to you.

- **Listen to her.** Let her talk. Do not interrupt. Do not try to defend yourself. Do not correct her. At this point, she is just trying to sort out her feelings; she may even make inaccurate and unreasonable accusations. It doesn't matter. Once she sees that you are really focusing on her, she will take them back and come to a more realistic view of the situation. When a woman sees that her partner is truly and patiently listening to her, she feels deeply supported and validated. It also helps if you nod encouragingly and say, "hmm" occasionally. Do this for as long as it takes. Forget the game you wanted to watch or lunch with your buddy. This is more important, it can save you days of resentment and heartache.

- **Ask her relevant questions.** Questions make a woman feel that you are paying attention and that you care about what she is feeling and thinking. Good questions, spoken gently and lovingly, include: "Which situations made you feel this way?" and "Could you explain to me why you think this?" These kinds of lead-ins allow her to vent more of her anger while also helping her start to look at the situation more calmly.

- **Think about what she is saying.** This may be the hardest part. It is difficult for anyone to look at their own behavior and decide that they have made a mistake or not handled something well. But you will earn great respect if you are able to admit that you have been wrong about something. Not always, not if you do not truly mean it. However, if you examine the situation, recognize that she has a point, explain to her how you have come to understand her feelings, and apologize, it is quite possible that the situation will instantly feel resolved to her.

- **Put yourself in her shoes.** To be completely satisfied, a woman is going to want to hear exactly how you came to the conclusion that her anger is justified. Think of how you might feel if she had done what you did. This will help you explain to her how you have come to understand her feelings.

- **Do not attack her.** When a person feels blamed, they often react defensively. Try to word things in terms of "I," rather than "you." Try to frequently use the word "feel." For instance, "When you did this, I felt this." Try to use emotion words, like "hurt," "sad," and "rejected." This will help her see you as a man who is strong enough to admit when he feels bad (and smart enough to use a woman's own language to communicate with her). It will also indicate to her that you trust and love her enough to share your vulnerability. This alone can go a long way towards calming her.

When She's Upset With You

- **Let past fights lie.** Do not use a current argument to rehash an old one, especially if that one was previously resolved. It only complicates the current issue while creating more anger and resentment.

- **Do not turn the tables.** Responding to her anger by raising unconnected issues, putting yourself down, or accusing her of wishing for a better partner, will only make things worse. She will feel that you are avoiding the problem. She will not be distracted. She will only become angrier. Saying that you aren't good enough for her, or a jerk, or whatever, will suggest to her that you are unwilling to try to improve your behavior. She will not feel sorry for you, or try to reassure you (at least, not after the first few times you try it), she will only get frustrated. In addition, if you hint that she no longer wants to be in a relationship with you, it will only lead her to start feeling insecure about *your* feelings for *her*.

- **Do not threaten to end the relationship.** If you are simply reacting to the situation, perhaps thinking that this is what she wants, it is sure to backfire on you. In most cases, she will not be arguing with you because she wants to break up, and rarely will she decide to break up during a disagreement. Women (and people in general) need to be able to express anger and work through issues. If you threaten the relationship every time, she will not feel comfortable enough to share her feelings with you. She will believe that if she gets angry with you then she runs the risk of losing you. This is not healthy for a relationship. Women get angry. It doesn't mean they don't want to be with you anymore. It means they want to improve the relationship. They also want to know that the relationship is important to you. If your response to any problem is to break up, or threaten to break up, rather than trying to resolve it, a woman will feel that you do not care that much about staying together. A woman needs to know that you will always fight to keep her.

Of course, if you have actually thought a great deal about breaking up and feel ready to do so, then go ahead. However, during a fight is not always the best time to implement such a decision.

- **Tell her how you feel** in a gentle and loving way. No doubt, this is very challenging for many men. However, it may be worth it. She will be so touched that you are opening up, and not getting angry at her for her feelings, that the rest of the conversation may flow much more smoothly. Beware, though, she may continue to rage at you for a little longer because she hasn't quite vented enough. Just listen and act understanding. She will soon cool off and marvel at how committed you are to her and to the relationship.

    And, if you are able to express your point of view in a kind way, and perhaps point out things that she may not have thought of, it's quite possible that she will actually listen to what you are saying and give it some consideration, perhaps even concluding that she has overreacted or misunderstood the situation. (This may be hard for you to conceive of, but give it a shot. What do you have to lose?)

- **Touch her.** Rub her back or her arm during the conversation. Even if she pushes you away. It tells her that you are there and present in every way, and that you love her even though you or she may be angry. It also reminds her of the wonderful and fulfilling parts of your relationship, so that while she is angry, a part of her will begin thinking more about her love for you than her anger.

- **Hold her.** When things have calmed down and you think it may be appropriate, take her in your arms. Do not suggest sex. Just cuddle and hold her.

- **Never reach for the remote, open your magazine, or ask, "Are we done?"** She will perceive these actions as a message that the whole incident was a waste of your time, you are just glad that it is about over, and you can't wait to get back to doing something *really* important. This may not be what you mean, of course, but it is what she *hears*. A more effective approach would be to ask her, "Do you feel like this is resolved?" or "Would you like to cuddle or should I turn on the television and we can watch together?"

- **Always tell her that you love her, how much she means to you, and how glad you are to have worked through this issue.**

When You're Upset

When You're Upset

- **Talk to her.** This is commonly understood as extremely difficult for men. However, if you don't, here are the possible consequences: 1) she will become certain you want to break up with her; 2) she will worry and wonder every second until you decide to explain; 3) she will talk to all of her friends about it to try to figure out what is wrong; 4) she will cry a lot; 5) she will feel rejected, abandoned, and alone; 6) she will bring it up again and again; and 7) she will not leave you alone. These are not exaggerations. She will feel and do all of these things painfully, powerfully, and repeatedly until the situation is somehow resolved for her.

- **Do not tell her "Nothing's wrong," or "I'll deal with it myself," or "It's no big deal."** This may be how you feel or you may just not want her to bother about it. No matter what the problem is, be it big or small, as long as you don't share it with her, she is going to have all of the reactions mentioned above. Even if it *is* no big deal. This is where John Gray may be wrong: it doesn't really help if you tell her, "I'm going into my cave for a while but I'll be back." She doesn't care if you will be back, you could be lying. She wants to know what the problem is right now or she is going to drive herself crazy. If she can sense that something is wrong and you are trying to hide it then she will feel as if something *really terrible* is going on. She will jump to the conclusion that it is about her, or that you don't trust her enough to share it with her. She's not asking so that she can help you work it out (though she may say that). She knows you can handle it yourself. She wants to know so that she doesn't have to worry. Or, if it is about her, then she wants to know so she can deal with it. As long as she doesn't know what the problem is, her mind will conjure up the worst possible explanations.

- **Try not to sulk.** You may find it useful to sulk, since it likely provokes a lot of attentive concern from her. However, what may seem like sweet (or perhaps annoying) consideration on her part can be a mask for other, less positive feelings. When a man is sullen, or quiet in a brooding kind of way, a woman begins to feel extremely insecure. Her response is to seek reassurance from the man. Many women learn to get a man's affirmation by going to great lengths to please him. This may be pleasant in the short run, but once things have worked out, a woman will often feel that she has been manipulated and used. If it happens repeatedly, she will begin to feel resentful, hurt, and angry whenever it occurs.

- **You can say "I'll tell you about it but then I want to deal with it by myself. I don't want to talk about it."** This WILL work. All she really wants to know is what is going on. If it is your problem and has nothing to do with her, she will probably not insist on dealing with it, if you don't want to. She may ask you about it now and again, but she will be easily put off by "I'm not ready to talk about it."

- **You can also say, "I don't want to talk about it right now, but I'll tell you about it in a little while."** Few women understand a man's need for space and time to work through whatever is going on for him. Women are very quick to see a rejection of themselves. But, if you tell her that you will share it with her at a specific future time, she may be able to be patient and give you the space you need. Just having your stated intention to tell her about it takes a lot of the fear out of the moment for her. It can help her keep herself calm and less worried about what you might be thinking if she knows that she will soon find out. This only works if you actually are able to tell her about it within a few hours or so. More than half a day will kick-start the previously mentioned reactions.

Jealousy and Double Standards

Jealousy and Double Standards

This section does not necessarily apply to all men. However, it may be useful to skim it, just in case.

There are many different levels of jealousy. This section does not address clinical possessiveness or obsession, only the milder, more common tendency to want to control a partner's behavior. The extent that partners allow each other to influence their day-to-day actions must be a decision made over time and with experience together, based on compromising and prioritizing, with each person's feelings taken into account.

A little jealousy may seem normal, just another part of being in a relationship with an attractive woman. If you find her attractive, then others must as well. Many women will even enjoy seeing their man behave a little possessively. Occasional displays can make a woman feel cherished and protected. You must be careful, however, if such attitudes become more than occasional. Few people enjoy feeling controlled, and many modern women will greatly resent attempts to dominate their actions.

It is also worthwhile for a man to understand that his concept of the effect a woman's behavior has on other men is different from hers. What you may think of as flirting, she may merely consider being friendly. It's true that she doesn't know men as well as you do, and doesn't see in their reactions what you see. However, she has also been dealing with them for as long as she has been alive. Be careful of judging her actions according to your beliefs, as opposed to hers.

- **Don't overreact if she smiles at another man.** Okay, maybe she's interested in him. Or maybe she just wants to tease him a little. Or maybe she's had it and is ready to dump you. But none of those things are likely. And you certainly can't come to any of those conclusions just because she smiles at someone. She probably smiles like that at other women, too. Most women smile much more readily than men. It's just a friendly reaction. For a woman, it rarely has to do with sex.

- **Don't overreact if she laughs with another man.** All of the above applies here, too. A woman can spend an entire evening having a great time with a man – your best friend, for instance, or her sister's husband – and never think about what kind of partner he would make, or what he is like in bed. Really.

- **Don't overreact if she sees a man when you aren't around.** Having lunch with a male co-worker, a friend's husband who needs some advice, or a childhood pal, is not usually a sign that your woman is having an affair. It is perfectly appropriate for a woman to have such outings. She likely does it because she is sociable and caring, not because she is thinking about getting into the sack with the guy. If it bothers you a lot, discuss it with her calmly, explain to her that it makes you uncomfortable, and ask her if she would be willing to respect your feelings about it.

- **Don't overreact if she hugs another man.** Many women are huggers. Because she hugs a man hello, or goodbye, or in sympathy, does not mean she is attracted to him. Maybe you're right and the man that's being hugged is getting a little thrill out of it. Chances are that your woman is not aware of it if he is (and may not even believe you if you tell her so). Physical affection can be entirely non-sexual for woman, believe it or not. So what if he's getting a thrill? You get the real thing.

- **Trust her.** Maybe you are not as concerned about what she is thinking as you are about what the guy is thinking. Try to remember that she probably has plenty of experience dealing with men in casual situations. If she is required to, she is likely to handle the guy just as you would wish.

- **Consider the rules you play by.** If she has done something that triggers your feelings of jealousy or insecurity, think about whether you've ever done something similar. If her old boyfriend called and she spoke to him for a few minutes, think about whether you've spoken to any old girlfriends since you've been in this relationship. If she has dinner with a male family friend, think about whether you've spent time with any female family friends. If she goes out with her coworkers for a drink after work, think about whether you've ever done that.

- **Explain what you see.** If there is a certain man in her life that makes you particularly uncomfortable, or if there is a certain way that she behaves around men that triggers your feelings of discomfort, try discussing it with her. If she sees that you are not simply generally jealous, but responding to something specific, she is more likely to take your feeling seriously and try to change.

- **Give her a class in Guys 101.** Many male reactions to women that you instinctively understand in a certain way have never even occurred to her. If you see a man behaving towards her in a manner that means something to you, something that warrants your protectiveness or jealousy, explain the behavior to your woman, clarify to her what you believe is going on in the man's mind. Educating her may be the fastest way to put an end to unhelpful behavior on her part, and may often result in her putting an end to any unhelpful behavior on another man's part.

Proposing

Proposing

- **If you are going to purchase a diamond ring for her,** try to get a sense of what she would like. Take her by a jewelry store and notice what she admires. If necessary, consult her best friend. Also,
    - Buy her a nice diamond. Listen to the salesman. Even if she has told you she doesn't care, she cares. And she will continue to care way past the proposal and long into the years of your marriage. Going into debt is not critical, but carefully consider how much you can spend: the more the better. They have payment plans. Take advantage of one. Think of it as an investment in your marriage, since that is precisely what it is.
    - This may go without saying, but just in case: do not, under any circumstances, use her money for the ring.

- **Do it well.** Some men (especially those who have already been given the go-ahead by their partner and are therefore assured of success) do not realize how critical the moment of proposal is to a woman. This is the moment she has been fantasizing about since she was ten. This is a moment she will remember for the rest of her life. This is the moment she will want to boast about to her friends, happily describe to her family, and proudly detail on her wedding website. Depending on the woman, it is probably only a slight exaggeration to say that, if you do not do it well, she may hold it against you for the rest of your life together. You will hear about it in twenty years when you have come home late from bowling (again) and she is crying "you don't love me enough to call, you didn't even love me enough to propose properly!" You'll see. It will haunt you.
    - Have flowers. Either red roses or her favorite blossoms.
    - Get down on your knees (yes, seriously).
    - Do it in a romantic spot: her favorite restaurant, the first place you went to together, a garden, a forest, a horse-drawn carriage... Do not do it in a house you share with her, at McDonalds, at the movie theatre, or anywhere else blah and disappointing.

- Try to be creative. Put the ring in a dish of her favorite ice cream, have her fortune cookie ask her to marry you, write your proposal on a bouquet of balloons, mow it on the lawn, put it into an ad in the newspaper, have a plane spell it across the sky...
- Dress well. Try to make it an evening when you would both dress up anyway, and do your best to look good (very good).
- If she says yes, order champagne or a nice bottle of wine. Tell her how happy she has made you.

Birthdays, Valentine's Day, Anniversaries, and Other Special Occasions

Birthdays, Valentine's Day, Anniversaries, and Other Special Occasions

These days are very important to a woman, probably beyond all sense, in your opinion. Nevertheless, in your constant and tireless effort to keep her happy and feeling loved, it is worthwhile for you to make it sincerely special. Even if it is early in your relationship, do not hesitate to take advantage of this opportunity to shine. These are her days to feel special and cherished, to be babied and pampered. Neglecting to go the distance on one of these days will cost you precious points, and probably result in having your partner feel unappreciated, unloved, unimportant, insecure, and generally unhappy with you, the relationship, and herself. One advantage you gain from pulling out all the stops is that some time later, when she is angry or upset about something that you have done, she will think back to her birthday, or your anniversary, or Valentine's Day, and remember your efforts. She will suddenly find herself filled with the knowledge that you really do care, the trouble of the moment miraculously forgotten.

Important dates when it is worthwhile to go the whole nine yards:

her 18th birthday, 21st, 30th, 40th, 50th, 60th, 65th, 70th, 75th, 80th, 85th, 90th, 95th, 100th, anything over that;

your 1st anniversary, your 10th, your 25th, your 50th, your 100th;

the day before she goes in for serious surgery;

the day she gives birth;

when she gets a raise or a promotion at work,

or pulls off a difficult presentation or project.

Each of these days must include certain crucial elements, but the details are up to you: a card, flowers, a loving phone call if you are not together, a gift, and some form of celebration (party, dinner, play...).

- **Do not forget.** (whether it is your 1 month or 1 year, her 23rd or 68th)

- **Plan ahead.** (And if you do not plan ahead, at least pretend to.) This suggests to her that she is so important to you that you want to put a great deal of thought and planning into making the day special for her. It also avoids mishaps (like not being able to find that sweater she wanted, no massages being available that day, or her favorite restaurant already booked solid).

- **Do not use her money.** If you share your income, then somehow save up the cash without her knowing. Do not use your shared credit card or account to pay for these days. In fact, try to keep her from having anything to do with the finances relating to her gifts or pampering.

- **Celebrate all day.** This does not necessarily mean that you have to get a day off from work, it just means little touches throughout the day.
    - have a card waiting by her bedside when she wakes up
    - surprise her with breakfast in bed
    - call her during the day to wish her a happy whatever
    - send her flowers
    - place little gifts or notes around the house for her to find.

    And if it is a day off for both of you, consider planning events for the entire day. Sample: Breakfast in bed with a rose and a card; a massage; a surprise road trip; a romantic dinner with candles and a gift, or a party.

- **If you are stressed out, don't let her know.** She wants to think that you enjoy doing these things for her (not that you do them because you know you will be in the doghouse if you don't). If you seem worried and frantic, she will feel like she is a burden to you and that you don't derive joy out of pleasing her. (This may be true, but it will not help your cause for her to know it.)

Birthdays, Valentine's Day, Anniversaries, and Other Special Occasions

- **Surprises are almost always a good idea.** <u>(Unless she doesn't like surprises – be sure to find out first)</u>. For a surprise to really be a surprise, she must know nothing, and suspect nothing. If she is the kind of woman that always needs to know everything about everything, then lie – this is the one time that you can get away with it. Do not, under any circumstances, let her know that anything is in the works. Women can be very smart and very particular. A surprise is not a surprise unless it is complete. This means planning the surprise portion as carefully as you plan the actual event. You must be extremely cunning. Her first inkling should come when she opens the door to the sound of "surprise!" or as you lead her into the restaurant or whatever it is you have planned. This cannot be stressed enough.

    - Do not let her hear you on the phone, or even indicate that you need to speak to someone privately.
    - Do not tell her fifteen minutes beforehand because you can't figure out how to get her to the restaurant. Think of something.
    - Do not say, "I can't tell you about that." Just lie. Convincingly. The more elaborately you keep the surprise from her, the more delighted she will be in the end.
    - Do not behave unusually in any way.
    - Consider pretending to have completely forgotten the special event (until the moment of revelation).

    Also, if there are kids or pets, then make arrangements for them. Nothing ruins a celebration for a woman more than suddenly realizing that her children or her animals are not being cared for. See later in this section.

- **Gifts.** (See **Surprises** above. Also see **Note What She Likes** in the **General Helpful Hints** section.) There must be a gift, no matter how small.

    Some good gifts:

- A homemade coupon book featuring actions you will perform when presented with a coupon (IOUs);
- gift certificates to her favorite stores;
- a song/poem/story you've written about her;
- a photo album featuring her from birth to adulthood;
- a scrapbook about her life or your life together;
- anything you have made yourself (but not something you have lying around, you have to make it specifically for her;
- clothes (only if you are absolutely <u>sure</u> that you know what she likes and her sizes);
- a professional massage or a personal massage (from you);
- a pampering day at the spa;
- a facial;
- jewelry (only if she likes it and if you are completely positive that you know her taste);
- books; and
- animals (if she likes them).

A cruise, a party, or dinner at her favorite restaurant are good celebrations but they are not enough as a gift. She must walk away from the day with a physical object that always will remind her of the day. And don't forget to wrap it and include a card. You may think those things are unimportant. She doesn't.

- **Flowers.** (Unless she is one of those women that doesn't believe in cut flowers – those women are rare, especially around Valentine's day, so don't assume). A wonderful (and inexpensive) method is picking, if possible, a large bunch of wildflowers, and placing them in a pretty vase (with water). If that is not an option, a dozen long-stemmed roses will always be appreciated. If this is out of range, or for variety, any bouquet (from an actual florist, not a grocery store) in a vase will do. One rose is okay, but not as great as many men

Birthdays, Valentine's Day, Anniversaries, and Other Special Occasions

seem to think. Never buy a woman white or black roses. An excellent trick, which will greatly please your partner, is sending them to her work. This way she has a chance to boast to her co-workers (not to mention any random women who wander in) and have them wishing their men were as thoughtful as you (or to look at it from a less cynical perspective: to allow her to share the beauty of your gift with her friends and have her feel attractive and desired by you even when you are apart).

- **Parties.** (See Surprises.) Parties can be good, especially if they are a surprise, or at least if you've done all the work and she hasn't had to do anything to make it happen. Just make sure to invite her friends, not only yours. Do not invite your buddy that she doesn't like (this is her day; he will understand better than she will). Be certain her name is spelled correctly on the cake (yes, if it is a birthday party, there needs to be a cake). Do not forget plates and plastic silverware and all the other necessities. Arrange the food beforehand, do not ask her what she wants once she arrives. What she wants is for all of the bases to have already been covered. Try to include treats she particularly likes.

- **Other Forms of Celebration.** (See Surprises) Women are different. You need to pay attention and try to get a sense of your particular woman's personal preferences.

  Some ideas include:
    - a picnic in a romantic spot (with food provided);
    - a homemade meal (with clean-up provided);
    - a play;
    - a murder mystery party or weekend;
    - dinner at her favorite restaurant;
    - a cruise;
    - an opera or concert;
    - a dance recital;

- a comedy club;
- a bed and breakfast;
- a weekend getaway;
- breakfast in bed; or
- a small get-together with her closest friends.

- **Pamper her.** Make plans for meals so she doesn't have to worry about them. Let her spend the morning in bed. Arrange for a manicure and pedicure. Kiss her all over.

- **Make it about her.** Especially if it's her birthday...
    - ask people to write little stories or poems about the first time they met her, or what they like the most about her, and put them in an album, a slide show, or a video
    - write something about her
    - have her friends help you make a collage of her
    - make a CD of her favorite songs, or songs that make you think of her

- **If she has kids or pets, make plans for them too, so that she can relax and enjoy** (or she will worry about them and it will spoil the party for her). Be sure the plans are ones she would have made herself. Don't send the kids to dear old deaf Aunt Zelda or grumpy Uncle Morty. Don't ask someone to just look in on the dog if the animal has never been left alone overnight before. Try to think what she would do.

- **If there are kids,** sometimes a nice gift for a mother is to take the kids somewhere for the day, allowing her some time to herself.

In Bed

In Bed

If you think you're a good lover because you have read lots of books, seen lots of movies, and had extensive conversations with your lovers about sexual technique, then you probably are. Therefore, you won't be at all embarrassed about reading this section. If you think you're a good lover because lots of women have told you so, then there's just no guarantee. That's just how it is. Women lie. They know how important it is to a man that he be considered a good lover. If it's a one-night stand, then what does she care, she can make him happy for one night. If it's a relationship, then she might just be hoping you'll eventually get better (miraculously), and doesn't want to ruin what sex life you do have together by making you feel insecure and self-conscious. If it's marriage, well, you'll know because she won't be interested in sex even three or four times a month (which is about what you can expect in a normal relationship that has lasted over five years), let alone more than once a week (which is what you get if you are <u>really</u> lucky). This section is not an exhaustive treatment of the topic. It also does not cover the vast variety of female preferences, styles, and interests. If you feel that you may need some help in this area, you would be wise to do some additional reading and research. Though unsatisfactory sex does not tend to be as devastating to a woman as it often is to a man, if it is consistent and long-term, it has the potential to destroy a relationship.

- **Try to smell good.** Brush your teeth. Use mouthwash. Shower within the day beforehand. (With soap.) Lovemaking is more pleasurable in the absence of unappealing odors.

- **Tease.** Many women love to be teased sexually. It is powerful foreplay for them. You can get a woman who is not at all in the mood ready and willing just by patiently and lovingly teasing her body. This means that you touch her slowly and gently all over, except where you mean to eventually touch. Get as close to her sensitive spots as possible, but do not actually go there. Keep this up for at least five minutes, ten to fifteen is even better. Then when she seems ready (or when she tells you that she is ready) wait just a little longer before putting your fingers (or whatever) where she wants them to go. Touch her for just a moment, then move away several times before you focus all of your attention on pleasuring that particular part of her. Do not use this method every time you make love. Once every three or four times should be sufficient.

- **Be gentle.** In general, this is good advice for all men. Many of you could stand to ease up a bit with your tongue, or finger, or toy. A woman wants to be caressed, not mauled; she wants to be stroked, not groped. Even if you do not think that you are physically abrasive, there is a good chance that you are. Stimulating a woman's clitoris is not done by rubbing it as fast as you can with your largest, most calloused finger. Many women do like it fast, but few like it fast and painful. Many men (particularly big, strong, macho ones) are not aware of how rough they can be. If you suspect you have such a tendency (and you might be able to find out by asking her), then think about how you touch your partner, then try to gentle it by at least ten times. See if she reacts. It is basically trial and error. Also, calloused hands, jagged fingernails, and stubbly chins can all significantly decrease your partner's pleasure, often leading to intense discomfort, and sometimes pain.

- **Make sure there is plenty of lubrication.** Do not underestimate the benefits of KY Jelly, Astroglide, or even more romantic oils, like scented or edible ones. To fully enjoy the sensations of sexual play, a woman needs to be extremely well lubricated. If in doubt, add more. Sometimes a woman's body produces the necessary lubrication, but more often (for various reasons, including hormonal changes, the position of the moon, what her day was like…) it will not. It is up to you to take note and remedy the situation. If you do not, intercourse may prove uncomfortable and irritating for her.

- **Pleasure her first,** as often as possible. One out of three women do not experience orgasms. It is your responsibility as a lover to bring your woman as close as possible as many times as you can. Find out if she has ever had one. Figure out the best possible way to get her there. Read a book on the subject, if necessary. They do exist.

- **But do not get carried away.** While it is critical to a woman that you be an attentive and considerate lover (this means focusing on her physical pleasure more than your own), she does not <u>always</u> have to orgasm to fully enjoy lovemaking. And it certainly is not critical that she orgasm at the same time as you. Despite all the hype, the truth is that a woman's sexual experience tends to be different from a man's; an orgasm is not always the ultimate satisfaction for her. Being caressed and titillated for a reasonable amount of time can sometimes be just as fulfilling. Placing too much importance on bringing her to climax will cause her to feel pressured to please you by climaxing. *This is why women sometimes fake it.*

- **Try new things.** Sex toys exist because they are fun. They do not replace you. They do not make you seem inadequate. They just add variety. In fact, if you are having trouble pleasing her, sometimes these tools can serve as a sure-fire way to accomplish your objective. Your partner is not likely to disrespect you, she is more likely to be impressed with your own security and determination to make her happy that you will attempt anything. Anything at all.

- **Be creative.** New positions can be awkward and silly, but they can also be incredibly pleasurable for women. Any position that involves something rubbing against her clitoris is going to be much appreciated and rewarded by greater satisfaction. Besides, women like it when men try to improve themselves.

- **Talk about it.**
    - If she is uncomfortable talking about your sex life, then she is probably nervous about how you might react to what she may say. Let her know how much you want to please her. Remind her that the only way you can become a better lover is by finding out how she likes to be touched. Be careful not to act hurt or defensive regardless of what she tells you.

- While you are talking, speak in a calm and loving tone of voice. Massage her back during the conversation. This tells her that you love her and are attracted to her despite whatever she might be saying.

- Ask her what she likes and doesn't like. If she tells you about something she doesn't like, <u>don't do it again</u>. Don't think, "Well, maybe she will like it this time." She won't. She will just be annoyed that you obviously were not paying attention when she told you the first time, or that maybe you are just more interested in your own satisfaction than hers.

- If she asks, tell her what you like. Try to focus on things she already does, then throw in one or two things that you would like to have her try. This will prevent *her* from feeling insecure or self-conscious.

• **Think variety.** Women get bored if you always want to do it in the evening, or always in the morning, or always at midnight. It *is* nice to go to sleep afterwards, but it can also be nice to go back to work in the afternoon with a big smile on your face. Also try different positions. Your body against hers stimulates different areas depending on how it is positioned. Women enjoy having different areas stimulated at different times, instead of everything always being the same.

• **It happens to all of you.** Really, it's okay, it's normal (except if it happens four out of five times, then you might want to seek professional help). In fact, by age 40, approximately 95% of all men have experienced episodes during which they do not ejaculate. All men have trouble every now and then. And it really isn't that big of a deal to her, except that maybe she is all hot and bothered and now you are so upset that you're not going to be into doing anything at all. Now, you're depressed and ashamed and you don't want to talk about it but, of course, you can't go to sleep now, no, you'll just go play your guitar or watch a game or something. Try to relax. She doesn't think any less of you as a man. She is not hurt, or angry, or amused. She is not suddenly thinking that you are permanently impotent. She will be just as happy if you put your arms around her and go to sleep cuddled up. The only way you actually wreck the evening is by getting so upset.

- **Don't feel rejected if she doesn't want to.** Some women just aren't interested in the same quantity of sex as men. It's not that she doesn't like it, she just doesn't like it as often. Think about it as your favorite food. If you had it every night, it would get boring, it wouldn't be your favorite anymore. In a sense, that is how some women think about sex. Spacing it out keeps it special and exciting. She also simply may not be in the mood at the same time as you. Try not to take it personally.

- **Don't pressure her.** A woman who feels pressured into having sex will not enjoy it. Therefore, if you have any hint that she is not really into it, you are better off dropping the subject. You may think that, "Aw, come on," or "You never want to do it anymore," or "It's been five days!" is harmless. It's not. She'll do it and she'll regret it. In fact, if you really want her to feel good and increase the chances of her wanting to the next evening (or even later that same night) then tell her, "it's okay, how about if we just cuddle?" Boy, she'll swoon for that one. (But you really have to *just* cuddle, without any undertones or roving hands).

Household

Household

Much of this is in the tradition of John Gray, but since usually only sensitive new-age men take the time to read John Gray, this may be helpful for you quick-fix kind of guys. Remember, especially with the following advice, it is much more effective if it is your idea, and if she hasn't already asked you to do it.

- **Take responsibility for some household cleaning.** It doesn't have to be a lot. Small things can make a big impression on a woman. Taking out the trash every day, or clearing the table; each lighten her work load, and may prevent her from feeling as if you never do anything around the house.

- **Don't reply "Food," or "I don't know"** if she asks what you would like for dinner. Recognize that preparing a meal is always an exercise in creativity and skill. A little help from you goes a long way.

- **Don't tell her that there is no milk (or whatever).** Write a note, or better yet, go pick it up yourself. Acting as if it is her primary responsibility to take care of your needs will make her feel unappreciated and taken for granted.

- **Go with her.** Shopping, the dry cleaner's, Walmart, wherever. Running errands with her will indicate that you enjoy spending time with her and that you know those errands are for your benefit, as well.

- **Do one extra household chore a week.** This is a good policy for keeping your woman happy, while not creating what you might consider unreasonable expectations. Taking out the trash will do, though vacuuming or mopping will be more noticeable. If there are chores you regularly do anyway, this chore should be something over and above, and it should be something different every week (so she does not start considering it your job). She will be constantly surprised and delighted, bragging to her friends, and generally considering you a better man than most.

- **Arrange for dinner once every two weeks.** This is only if you do not normally do the cooking. If you usually do dinner, then surprise her with breakfast (in bed is highly preferable). Be sure to include a main dish, a starch (potatoes, rice, bread), and a vegetable. If you are not much of a cook, it doesn't matter. In this case, it is definitely the thought that counts: spending time and effort on a woman is a meaningful way to demonstrate your love and caring (just ask her). However, do not leave a messy kitchen for her to deal with. That will just defeat your original purpose.

- **If the kitchen is her domain,** do not attempt to help her by rearranging things. If you use something, put it back in its place.

- **Help her out.** Now and then pick a task that she usually does and do it for her (like making the kids' lunches or your own, or doing the grocery shopping, or feeding the pets).

- **Clean up after yourself.** Put your clothes in the hamper, including your socks. Fold and re-hang your towel. Clothes lying around tend to make a woman feel unappreciated and taken for granted. Even though you probably fully intend to take care of them yourself at some later date, her impression is going to be that she is expected to walk around after you picking up your messes as if you were her child instead of her husband. It is in your best interest to avoid this unpleasant misunderstanding.

- **If you're having guests (especially ones that you've invited), tidy up around the house.** Or at least help her if she's doing it. Offer to assist with dinner or other preparations.

- **Clean the whole house (thoroughly).** It is probably best to save this for once a year, or, at the most, every six months. This is a big one, for you effort-wise, and for her pleasure-wise. It is a lot of work and you want to make sure she will be gone for the whole day or weekend that it will take you. Remember that her reaction will be worth it. You'll see. She will never forget that you did it, and you will reap the benefits for many months (or even years).

- **Thank her for the things she does "normally."** Even if she does the dishes every night, or cleans the house every week, or makes breakfast every day, she will feel appreciated if you take notice. No matter how often you let her know how grateful you are for the things she does, it will always make her day.

Small Things That Men Are Often Unaware Of
(They won't earn you that many brownie points, but not doing them will quickly put you in the doghouse)

- Always put the toilet seat down.
- Always replace the toilet paper when you've used that last little square.
- **Take the trash out when it's full.** (And always replace the trash bag.)
- **Turn the TV off if you leave the room** (providing she isn't watching it.)
- Consult her before you channel surf.
- Keep the noise down when she's sleeping.

General Helpful Hints

General Helpful Hints

- **Listen to her.** Though this has been mentioned before, it cannot be stressed enough. The best way to let a woman know you care is by listening to her and asking questions about what she is saying. Not like, "what did you just say?" More like, "what made you feel that way?" or "and then what happened?" Women like to talk; it helps them work through their feelings or put life in perspective. When a man they love (or even just like) listens to them (all the little details, even things that seem completely unimportant), they eventually feel as if everything is going to be okay, their relationship is incredible, they are attractive and charming women, and they just love you so much.

- **Note what she likes.** When she points out or mentions something she would like to have (or do), make a note of it (later, when she can't see you). Then surprise her with it on a birthday or anniversary, or even just out-of-the blue. She will be touched that you are so sensitive to her that you remember even some casual comment she made two months ago. (This list will also be immeasurably helpful to you during those times when you are actually required to come up with a gift).

- **Bring her presents.** Not every week, because then it gets old, and expected. Try for once every two months, just to let her know that you are always thinking about her (and that it doesn't take a special occasion to make you want to do something for her). Again, such gifts do not need to be expensive. Women love it when you write a little note on a card, or give something else that took thought and effort. You can pick up a box of her favorite chocolates, a bouquet of flowers, a single red rose, a scarf she's been wanting, a romantic book… Also, try for a variety. Flowers every week or month become commonplace, and feel more like a duty than a pleasure (to both of you). Always remember to remove price tags.

- **Watch her TV shows with her.** You don't have to do it constantly. Just now and then, turn to a show you know she likes, and sit with her while she enjoys it. This will be enough to make her feel that her needs and preferences are just as important to you as your own.

- **Cuddle with her.** Many men do not understand how significant cuddling can be to a woman. If the only time you touch her is when you want to get her into bed, your partner is probably suffering from the "sometimes I think he only wants me for sex" complex. Hug her once a day, without any sexual undertones. Rub her back while you are watching TV together. Kiss her cheeks and her forehead when you are lying in bed. Hold her. Hold her as often as you can. All her insecurities will melt away.

- **Tell her about it.** Take Billy Joel's advice. He had it right. Tell her that you love her. Tell her what you appreciate about her. Tell her how important she is to you. This may all seem unnecessary to you but it means a great deal to a woman (especially if you are not the talkative type; then she knows you really mean it). She will cherish your words for hours, sometimes days or weeks.

- **If she has kids,** accompany her to their activities. Watching her son's football game or her daughter's dance recital (or vice-versa) can win you infinite brownie points.

- **Include her family in your life.** Accepting and spending time with her family, especially her kids, is often a sure way to a woman's heart.

Conclusion

Well, good luck sir. Just the fact that you've shown any interest in this book is a mark in your favor. Even trying out one or two suggestions described here could have a profound impact on your relationship.

Perhaps you find some or most of the recommendations emasculating, ridiculous, or simply too much to ask. Did your partner or some well-meaning female friend present this to you as a gift? Consider seriously before dismissing it all as just a load of... well, whatever. Remember that your concept of what is important, valid, and worthwhile is determined by less than half of the population. This book may make it seem as if it's up to you to do all of the work, but maybe it will actually help you see how much it is your partner really does. And maybe, with your new insight and assistance, you'll find your partner giving to you more than ever in the ways in which you truly want to be given. The ideas expressed here may serve you well, with rewards both unpredictable and unexpected. And, after all, is there more to lose or more to gain by trying them?

Or maybe you're thrilled to finally have an instruction manual for your partner. If that's where you're coming from, then you're to be applauded. A wonderful man you are and soon she will see that even more clearly. It takes a lot of love, courage, and strength to change yourself, and to seek a deeper understanding of your partner. She's very lucky to have you.